DENNIS YE MENACE
AND HIS TRUSTY SQUIRE, GNASHER

LES PRETEND

So—

THE BABYSITTING AGENCY SENT ROUND THIS COOL YOUNG LADY.

SHE SAID "MY NAME'S MISS PILKINGTON BUT YOU CAN CALL ME SADIE."

WHEN MUM WENT OUT YOUNG LARRY SCREAMED "HOI — GET A MOVE ON — QUICK!"

READ ME A BEDTIME STORY OR I'LL SCREAM UNTIL I'M SICK!"

"I DON'T WANT BORING NURSERY RHYMES THAT ANCIENT TRASH I HATE."

THE GIRL SAID "LISTEN, KID AND I WILL BRING THEM UP TO DATE."

THE LITTLE BRAT WENT CRAZY, WHEN SADIE TOLD HIM "HUSH!"

HOLLER! BAWL! RANT! RAVE!

A BOWL OF "BABY-DOLLOP" WENT "SPLAT!" RIGHT IN HER MUSH!

SPLAT!

CHUCK!

HER CRUCIAL THREADS WHERE RUINED, SHE REALLY GOT DISTRESSED

SPLATTERED! SLABBER!

DRIBBLE!

MALEVOLENT! MIRTH!

WHEN LUMPS OF HORRID SLIMEY GUNGE SLITHERED DOWN INSIDE HER VEST!

DRIP! PLOP!

HORRIBLE SLIMY SLITHERINGS DEEP IN THE DRAWERS!

NOW I'D SUGGEST YOU TURN THE PAGE IN A COUPLE OF SECONDS TIME . . .

STEAM!

GNAARSH! GRIND!

UNLESS YOU WANT TO WITNESS A HORRIBLE "NURSERY-CRIME!!"

DIABOLICAL DASTARDLY DEEDS ABOUT TO BE DONE!

EXTREME CASE OF THE WILLIES!

CLUTCH!

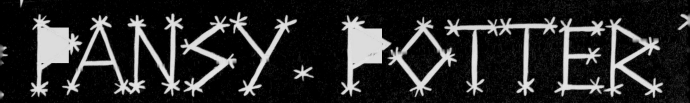

PANSY POTTER

THE STRONG MAN'S DAUGHTER

GENERAL JUMBO

JUMBO JOHNSON had his own private army, navy and airforce — fabulous models built by his friend Professor Carter. Jumbo was putting on a mock battle in the grounds of Dinchester Comprehensive to raise funds for his school.

...AND NOW AS THE NAVAL BOMBARDMENT LIFTS, THE ALLIED COMMANDER CALLS FOR AN AIR-STRIKE AS HIS LANDING CRAFT HEAD FOR THE BEACHES!

ALLIED TROOPS COME UNDER MACHINE-GUN FIRE AS THEY STORM THE BEACHES.

ONE BY ONE THE ENEMY GUNS ARE SILENCED.

THREE CHEERS FOR JUMBO JOHNSON! HIP, HIP...

HURRAY!

SAVE·OUR·SCHOOL

The headmaster thanked Jumbo—

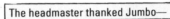

AS YOU ALL KNOW, OUR SCHOOL IS BADLY IN NEED OF REPAIR AND DINCHESTER COUNCIL ARE UNABLE TO HELP US. I HAVE TO TELL YOU THAT AN OFFER HAS BEEN MADE TO BUY THE BUILDING AND DEMOLISH IT IN ORDER TO BUILD A SUPERMARKET.

New sports equipment was installed in the school gym with the money, but the next morning . . .

THIS IS HEARTBREAKING! ALL OUR NEW EQUIPMENT HAS BEEN DESTROYED!

THE PUPILS WE HAVE SPOKEN TO SEEM RELUCTANT TO ASSIST US.

SOUNDS LIKE A JOB FOR ME!

Jumbo set up a secret control room in the school grounds.

OPEN UP, PROFESSOR. IT'S JUMBO!

THIS IS REALLY EXCITING!

THE MODELS ARE SO LIFE-LIKE!

AND FINALLY THE ISLAND IS SECURED!

WELL DONE! A WONDERFUL SHOW!

ORDER PLEASE! IF OUR SCHOOL IS TO BE SAVED WE NEED MORE PUBLIC-SPIRITED PEOPLE LIKE JUMBO JOHNSON TO COME FORWARD AND HELP US!

NO! NEVER! SAVE OUR SCHOOL!

YOU HAVE ONE HERE, HEADMASTER!

WHAT'S THIS?

CHARLES DENVER'S THE NAME — LOCAL BUSINESSMAN. PERHAPS THIS CHEQUE FOR ONE THOUSAND POUNDS WILL HELP?

BRAVO!

NOBODY SUSPECTS THIS TELEVISION REPAIR VAN IS ACTUALLY OUR CONTROL ROOM, PROFESSOR. NOW TO KEEP WATCH.

CARTER REPAIRS & SERVICE

ALL QUIET SO FAR, JUMBO.

LOOKS LIKE WE'VE GOT A CASE OF BULLYING IN PROGRESS OUTSIDE THE WEST GATE, JUMBO!

A JOB FOR MY SQUADRON!

But Jumbo found Tommy and Kenny reluctant to talk about their trouble.

Jumbo returned to the control room.

CONTINUED LATER IN THE BOOK.

GNASHER and GNIPPER

DOGS ARE DIFFERENT SHAPES AND SIZES ACCORDING TO WHAT THEY'RE MEANT TO DO, SON.

GREYHOUNDS ARE SKINNY SO THAT THEY CAN RUN FAST.

BUTCHER

WATCH THESE SOSSIES

SNAP

SLOBBER

AND DACHSHUNDS ARE SHORT, SO THEY CAN HUNT UNDER BUSHES.

SAUSAGE SMELL

YAP! YIP!

BULLDOGS ARE LIKE THAT BECAUSE THEY'RE TOUGH.

GROOF!

YEEK!

IVY the TERRIBLE

Soon— HUMPH! I'D LIKE TO ORDER!

I'LL HAVE TO GET THE WAITER'S ATTENTION! CHUCKLE!

THUD!

OUCH!

BASH!

I SAY! LOOK OUT!

OO . . . ER! SORRY, SIR!

LOOK AT MY WIG — COVERED IN SOUP! HUMPH!

HA HA HA

I'LL HAVE SAUSAGE, CHIPS AND LOTS OF PEAS, MY GOOD MAN!

Shortly—

SUPER! I HATE PEAS!

BUT THEY'RE GREAT FOR FIRING!

OW!

OUCH!

HELP!

PING!

PING!

HERE'S THE BILL! PAY UP AND LEAVE!

BURP!

NO PROBLEM!

I'VE GOT LOTS OF CASH IN MY PIGGY BANK!

Behold the Orangutangaroo,
The weirdest creature in my zoo.
It bounces high and swings from trees,
It has a tail and hairy knees.
On days that I am late for school —
Which are quite often as a rule,

He shoves me in his pouch — it's fine —
And bounces there before it's nine.
Beware the Orangutangaroo,
It can be dangerous — it's true.
Although it may look so appealing,
It tends to devastate your ceiling.

SIDNEY'S ZOO

A wondrous beast is the Smellyphant,
Through Dad's garden it lumbers along.
It eats ancient socks and garlic filled chocs
Which might well account for the pong.
The niff that exudes from a Smellyphant
Makes giant apes fall in a swoon.

It finds it quite easy to make skunks feel queasy,
It's said the pong reaches the moon.
I pity the foul-scented Smellyphant —
Well how would *YOU* feel if you stunk?
But he's not so thick, he's got a smart trick —
He ties a large knot in his trunk.

BALLBOY

NOW TO SCORE!

HOI! WHAT ARE YOU DOING IN MY RASPBERRY NETS?

GET LOST!

HMM! HAVE TO FIND A WAY TO SEE.

So —

THESE MINERS' HELMETS WILL DO THE TRICK.

EXCEPT THEY GET BLACKED OUT IF YOU HEAD A MUDDY BALL!

THERE'S ONLY ONE THING FOR IT . . .

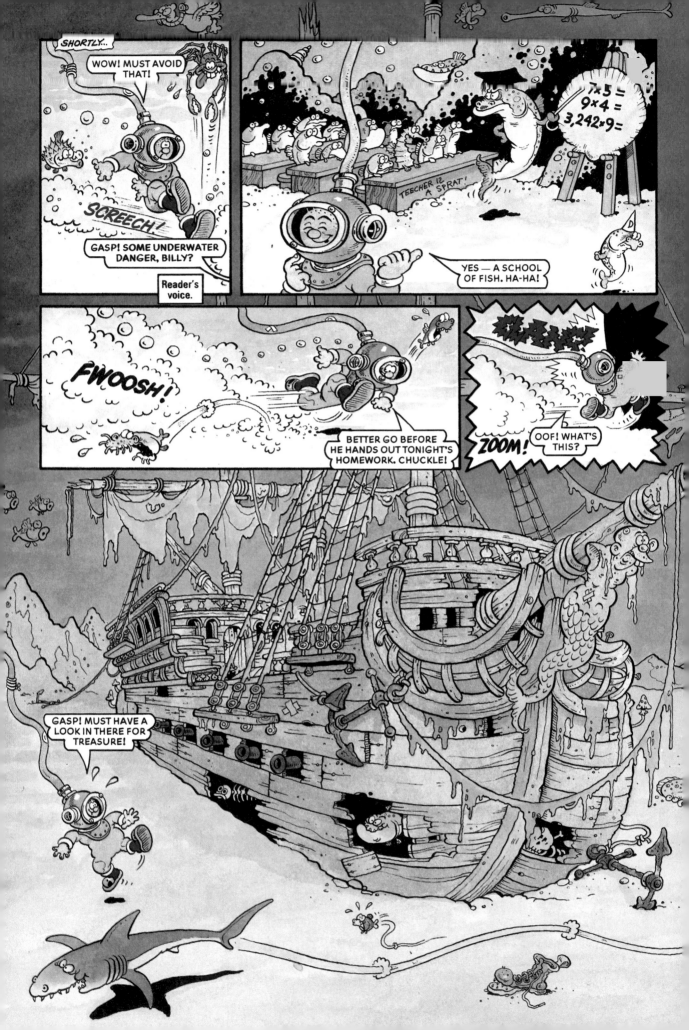

INSIDE...

GREAT FUN!

SWAG

BUT THEN...

EH? WHO ...?

WHO'S THIS WHO COMES TO VISIT KING NEPTUNE?

ER ... I'M BILLY WHIZZ! I THOUGHT YOU WERE ONLY ON THE PAGES OF STORY BOOKS!

HO-HO!

NEP

SO DID I THINK THAT OF YOU, BILLY! I'M A BEANO FAN!

THE BEANO

THE REAL TREASURE

WELL I NEVER!

THANKS, ROGER!

WHAT SHALL WE DO WITH THIS MONEY?

JINGLE!

GO TO THE CINEMA? OKAY, ARCHIE!

NOW SHOWING
LETHAL BANANA
STARRING —
MEL GIBBON.

ROXY CINEMA

NO PETS ALLOWED

SORRY, ARCHIE — NO PETS ALLOWED IN.

I'VE AN IDEA, THOUGH!

ONE TANK DAMAGED, PROFESSOR! THREE MEN WOUNDED AND ONE AIRCRAFT MISSING!

The following night.

KEEP DOWN, LADS! JUMBO JOHNSON'S PATROL PLANE WON'T SPOT US THIS TIME!

Jumbo's fire-fighter kept the fire under control until Dinchester fire brigade arrived.

LEAVE IT TO THEM NOW, JUMBO!

SCIENCE LAB

And the next morning . . .

WE'D LIKE TO KNOW HOW THE FIRE STARTED!

MY ENTIRE FORCE HAS BEEN IMMOBILISED, PROFESSOR! SOMEONE MUST HAVE PLANTED THAT DAMAGED PLANE IN THE LAB!

I CAN BUILD A DUPLICATE ARM-CONTROL, JUMBO — BUT IT WILL TAKE TIME!

The professor worked feverishly.

IT'S MIDNIGHT, PROFESSOR! I'M CERTAIN THE VANDALS WILL LAUNCH ANOTHER ATTACK TONIGHT!

NEARLY FINISHED, JUMBO!

While outside . . .

GO TO IT, BOYS! JUMBO JOHNSON'S ARMY WON'T HINDER YOU TONIGHT!

IT'S WORKING, PROFESSOR!

AND JUST IN TIME! INTRUDERS IN THE LOWER SCHOOL!

WE'LL REALLY SMASH THE PLACE UP TONIGHT, LADS!

BILLY, LOOK!

And later . . .

THE SCHOOL LAB, JUMBO!

I'LL ALERT FIRE CONTROL!

I SAW JUMBO JOHNSON FOOLING AROUND IN HERE WITH HIS MODEL AIRFORCE, HEADMASTER!

WHAT'S THIS?

MY MISSING PLANE!

Jumbo was questioned by the police.

YOU'RE MAKING A MISTAKE, SIR! I DIDN'T START THAT FIRE!

I'M SORRY, JUMBO, BUT ONE OF YOUR MODEL PLANES WAS FOUND THERE.

FOLLOW ME, LADS!

DINCHESTER COMPREHENSIVE SCHOOL.

WHERE DID THEY COME FROM! AARGH!

WE'RE SURROUNDED! CALL 'EM OFF!

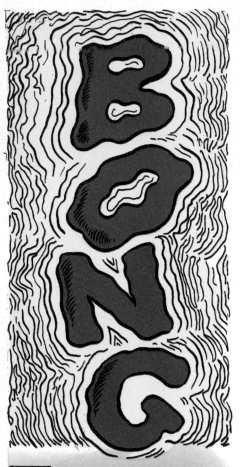

THE NIBBLERS

Enor | Scritch and Scratch | Gordon Zola | Cheddar George | His Nibs | Chiseller | Sniffler

SSH! WHISKERS IS SLEEPING AGAIN!

CREEP!

SHOULDN'T WE SHARE WITH WHISKERS?

GOOD IDEA!

Whiskers

FIRST WE TIE HIS WHISKERS!

Porky

PULL!

PULL BACK . . .

PLUSH!

. . . THEN LET GO!

BAH! MY LARDER'S BEEN RAIDED GAIN!

BIKS

FAR TOO MANY CAT NAPS, YOU LAZY CAT!

GLOOM!

THIS'LL KEEP YOUR EYES OPEN AND STOP YOU SLEEPING ON DUTY!

Meanwhile—

I'M GOING TO PAINT WILL'S TONGUE RED!

But—

WAH!

GREAT! OUR POGO STICKS HAVE GOT RED PAINT ON THEM!

LET'S GO OUTSIDE!

WAHEY!

YAWN!

WAH! I MUST HAVE MEASLES!

SO REMEMBER, READERS — THE BEST WAY TO STOP MEASLES IS TO PINCH YOUR GERMS' POGO STICKS!

MISSING!

HELP TEACHER TRACK DOWN THE KIDS IN THIS FUN TO PLAY GAME. ANY NUMBER CAN COMPETE. USE COUNTERS, BUTTONS OR EVEN JELLY BABIES AS MARKERS — YOU'LL NEED A DICE TOO. FOLLOW THE INSTRUCTIONS ON THE SQUARE YOU LAND ON. (IF THIS INSTRUCTION TELLS YOU TO MOVE FORWARD OR BACK, IGNORE THE INSTRUCTION ON THE SQUARE YOU'RE SENT TO.) YOU MUST FINISH EXACTLY ON SQUARE 22. IF YOU ARE ON SQUARE 19 FOR EXAMPLE AND THROW A FIVE, YOU MOVE THREE SPACES FORWARD THEN TWO BACK (TOTAL FIVE), TO FINISH ON THE DREADED SQUARE 20. HAVE FUN!

3 HIT BY GIANT SNOWBALL THROW A SIX BEFORE YOU CAN START AGAIN.

4 NOBODY TO BE SEEN MOVE ON TO NEXT SQUARE ONLY.

5 HEAR THE PING OF ELASTIC. TAKE ANOTHER TURN.

8 FOOTPRINTS LEAD TO SNOWMAN NOT KIDS. GO BACK ONE PLACE ONLY.

7 PUZZLED BY STRANGE FOOTPRINTS IN THE SNOW. MISS A TURN.

6 SNOWBALL MISSES YOU. GO ON TO SQUARE NINE ONLY.

15 SCARED BY POLAR BEAR. GO ON ONE SQUARE ONLY.

16 AVOID LAUGHING HYENAS. GO ON ONE SQUARE ONLY.

17 PECKED IN THE TROUSERS BY PENGUINS. GO BACK TO FOURTEEN ONLY

20 NO SIGN OF THE KIDS. START AGAIN.

19 BUS GETS LOST IN SNOW. THROW A ONE TO RESTART.

18 ESCORTED TO BUS STOP BY HELPFUL GORILLA. GO ON TO TWENTY ONLY.

The BRAT

Dennis and Gnasher

SPLURGE

SPLAT

SPLAT

YEUCH! STOP THAT, DENNIS!

AW! YOU'RE SPOILING MY FUN, DAD!

LIFT

HUMPH! WHY CAN'T YOU BE A NICE BOY, LIKE WALTER?

HUH!

WALTER PRINCE OF SOFTIES ↓

SKIP

SNARL! IF DAD WANTS A 'WALTER' — HE'S GOING TO GET ONE!

SWOON

GOOD! THIS NEW TALL FENCE WILL BE WORTH EVERY PENNY TO KEEP DENNIS AND GNASHER OUT OF MY GARDEN!

THUD THUD

Dennis's neighbour.

But —

NO NEED, MISTER NEIGHBOUR. I'LL NOT KICK MY SOFT SPONGE BALL NEAR YOUR GARDEN!

FLUMP

RAGE

SNARL! ALL THAT MONEY — WASTED!

FLUMP

ARMY CAMP

TUM-TEE-TUM!

OKAY, MEN! BRACE YOURSELVES FOR YOUR 'TOUGHNESS TEST'!

OO . . . ER!

WAH!

BIFF

KICK

KICK

DENNIS REALLY PUTS THEM THROUGH THEIR PACES!

NOT TODAY! WE'RE PRACTISING OUR BALLET STEPS!

EH?

GASP!

LEAP

THE MENACE HAS GONE — SOFT!

WE WANT OUR MENACE BACK!

STOP HIM GOING SOFT!

So —

ER . . . WELL! I THINK DENNIS HAS CHANGED SO MUCH — HE'LL NEVER GO BACK TO BEING A MENACE!

But —

YOU THINK SO! HAR-HAR!

TWANG!

YAHOO SOOT CUSTARD BRVAT SOOT BRVTH

AAARGH!

GLOOF!

CUSTARD SOOT SOOT CUSTARD

Then —

YAHOO! THE MENACE IS BACK!

HA-HA! A GREAT PLAN TO STOP COMPLAINTS ABOUT MY MENACING FOR A WHILE!

ZOOM

BLAT

SPLAT

OO . . .! I'M SO ANGRY THE MENACE IS BACK — I COULD TEAR A WET PAPER HANKIE IN TWO! HUMPH!

FINISH

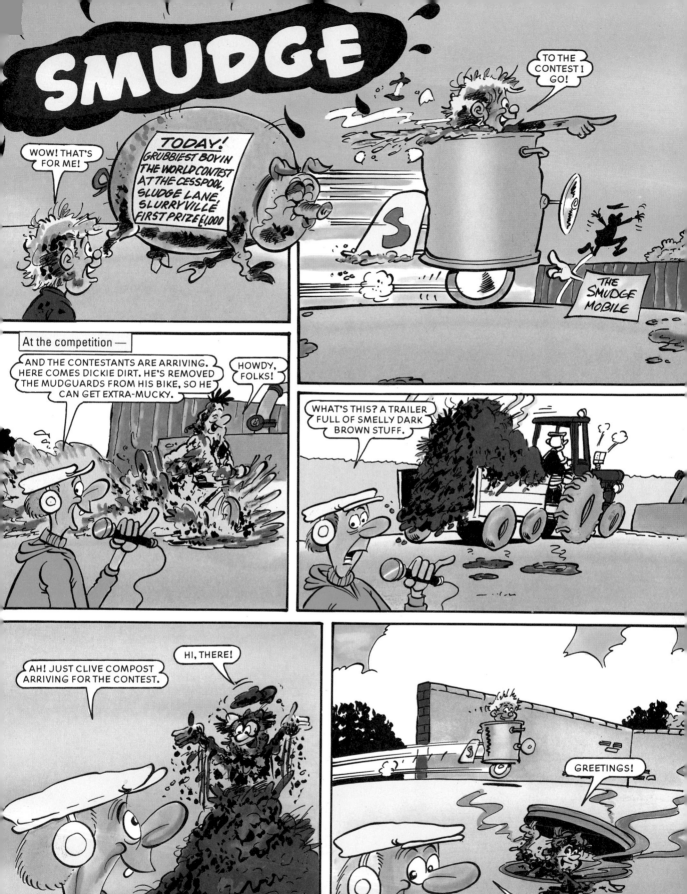

HURRY UP, SMUDGE!

DON'T BE DAFT. THE SLOWER I AM THE MORE TIME I HAVE IN THIS LOVELY GUNGE.

After the final contest —

AND SMUDGE WITH HIS ELASTIC TROUSERS WINS THE TURNIPS DOWN YOUR PANTS CONTEST.

So —

YOU'RE THE WINNER, SMUDGE, AND HERE'S YOUR £1000 CHEQUE. WELL DONE — YOU WERE ABSOLUTELY DISGUSTING!

WOW! BRILLIANT!

At Beanotown Bank —

I'LL CASH THIS CHEQUE AND BUY MY VERY OWN RUBBISH TIP.

I WANT TO CASH THIS HERE CHEQUE, MISTER BANK PERSON.

CASH IT? I CAN'T EVEN READ IT IT'S SO MUCKY. PUSH OFF!

THIS IS THE REAL LISTENING BANK. WE'VE LISTENED.

....NOW SHOVE OFF

MUTTER! SOMETIMES BEING MUCKY ISN'T SO CLEVER.

The hippopotamouse it's said
Would fill the bravest man with dread.
You wouldn't like it — not at all,
If one made holes in your nice wall.
If it was chased by some daft cat,
The brute would squash the moggie flat.

And you'd be deafened for a week
If it should let out one loud SQUEAK!
The beast would guzzle tons of cheese
And cause destruction with one sneeze.
If you leave crumbs around the house,
BEWARE THE HIPPOPOTAMOUSE!

AT SIDNEY'S ZOO

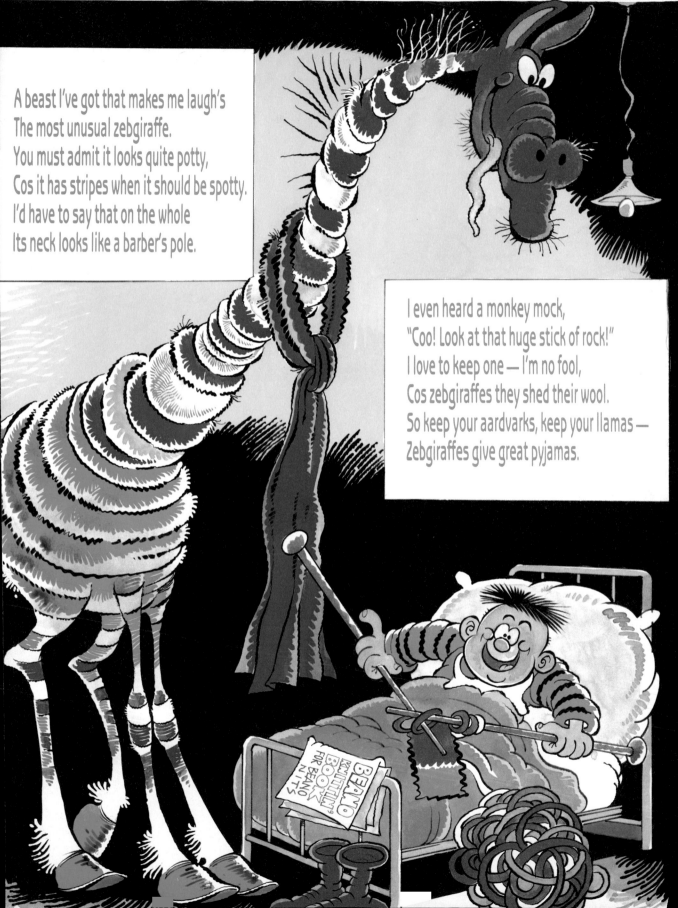

A beast I've got that makes me laugh's
The most unusual zebgiraffe.
You must admit it looks quite potty,
Cos it has stripes when it should be spotty.
I'd have to say that on the whole
Its neck looks like a barber's pole.

I even heard a monkey mock,
"Coo! Look at that huge stick of rock!"
I love to keep one — I'm no fool,
Cos zebgiraffes they shed their wool.
So keep your aardvarks, keep your llamas —
Zebgiraffes give great pyjamas.

TOOOOOT

I FORGOT TO MENTION . . .

. . . WE DO GET A BIT BUSY WHEN THE BUILDING SITE STOPS FOR LUNCH. HA-HA!

2 × 2

POUND

So —

WE KNOW A SAFER PLACE WITH A BLACKBOARD, TEACHER.

TWITTER!

Soon —

THIS PLACE HAS A SUPER BLACKBOARD . . .

2 × 2

. . . BUT TEACHING IN A TOY SHOP HAS ITS DISTRACTIONS.

ZOOM

2 × 2 =

SALE £25

QUICK SETTING CLAY

BUMP

CRUNCH

MEE—MAW